This
NO...
ELEPHANT JOKE BOOK
belongs to

_____

Also available in Beaver by John Hegarty
A VERY MICE JOKE BOOK

NOT THE ELEPHANT JOKE BOOK

John Hegarty

Illustrated by David McKee

Beaver Books

A Beaver Book
Published by Arrow Books Limited
62-5 Chandos Place, London WC2N 4NW

An imprint of Century Hutchinson Ltd

London Melbourne Sydney Auckland
Johannesburg and agencies throughout the world

First published 1987

Text © Martyn Forrester 1987
Illustrations © Century Hutchinson Ltd 1987

This book is sold subject to the condition that it shall not, by way of trade or otherwise, be lent, resold, hired out, or otherwise circulated without the publisher's prior consent in any form of binding or cover other than that in which it is published and without a similar condition including this condition being imposed on the subsequent purchaser.

Set in Century Schoolbook
by JH Graphics Ltd, Reading

Made and printed in Great Britain
by Anchor Brendon Ltd
Tiptree, Essex

ISBN 09 951040 5

For Ben

This way in

Congratulations for visiting **Not the Elephant Joke Book**.

Clearly you are not all grey and wrinkled like those sad jumbo dumbos who still go around telling elephant jokes.

If you know any of these poor jokers (easily recognizable by their extremely large ears and long noses), please give them a copy of this book at once – then put them in touch with us here at The Royal Society For The Prevention Of Cruelty To Animal Jokes.

We have highly trained people, many of them ex-elephants themselves, who can tell brilliant jokes about every creature from aardvarks to zebras (except YOU-KNOW-WHATS) – until the cows come home . . .

A mixed bag of knock knock jokes

Knock, knock.
Who's there?
Alpaca.
Alpaca who?
Alpaca picnic lunch.

Knock, knock.
Who's there?
Gopher.
Gopher who?
Gopher your gun, sheriff.

Knock, knock.
Who's there?
Weasel.
Weasel who?
Weasel while you work.

Knock, knock.
Who's there?
Yukon.
Yukon who?
Yukon lead a horse to water, but you can't make him drink.

Knock, knock.
Who's there?
Ralph.
Ralph who?
Ralph! Ralph! Ralph! I'm your new puppy dog!

Another mixed bag

What do you get if you cross a hyena with an Oxo cube?
A laughing stock.

What animal would you like to be on a cold day?
A little otter.

CUSTOMER: Can I have some rat poison please?
CHEMIST: *Have you tried Boots?*
CUSTOMER: I want to poison them, not kick them to death!

What did Santa say to his wife on Christmas Eve?
Don't go out in the reindeer.

Ant jokes

Where do tourist ants go?
Frants.

What do ants put under their arms?
Antiperspirant.

What is the leader of the ants called?
The Presidant.

Where does a silly ant live?
Antwerp.

What is small and hairy and has six legs?
An ant with a fur coat on.

Bat jokes

What animal is the best cricket player?
The bat.

What happened to the two mad vampires.
They went bats.

What does a bat sing in the rain?
'Raindrops Keep Falling On My Feet.'

VAMPIRE VICTIM: A vampire bat bit me on the neck last night.
FRIEND: *Did you put anything on it?*
VICTIM: No, it seemed to like it as it was.

What do vampire bats eat for breakfast?
Ready Neck.

Bear jokes

What's yellow, comes from Peru, and is completely unknown?
Euston Bear.

What do you get if you cross a grizzly bear with a harp?
A bear-faced lyre.

What do you call a bald koala?
Fred Bear.

Why was Goldilocks from such a small family?
Because she had three bears but everyone else has forebears.

Bee jokes

'I've just been stung by one of your bees.'
'Show me which one, and I'll punish it.'

Why do bees fly around crossing and uncrossing their back legs?
They're looking for a BP station.

What did the mother bee say to the baby bee?
'Don't be naughty, honey, just beehive yourself while I comb your hair.'

'Doctor, doctor, I think I'm a bee.'
'I'm busy myself – buzz off.'

What is the difference between a sick tiger and a dead bee?
One is a seedy beast, and the other is a bee deceased.

Bird jokes

JOHN: Mum's got a tweet in store for my birthday.
PAUL: *A tweet? Don't you mean a treat?*
JOHN: No, I mean a tweet. She's getting me a budgie!

What do a toucan, a pelican and a taxman all have in common?
Big bills!

Did you hear about the idiot who did bird impressions?
He ate worms!

Knock, knock.
Who's there?
Wendy.
Wendy who?
Wendy red, red robin comes bob, bob, bobbin' along . . .

Buffalo and bison jokes

What's the difference between a buffalo and a bison?
You can't wash your hands in a buffalo.

What did the buffalo say to his son when he left on a long journey?
'Bison.'

What do you call a 200-year-old buffalo?
A bison-tenary.

What kind of buffalo has four legs but cannot walk?
Roast buffalo.

Camel jokes

What do you get if you cross a cow with a camel?
Lumpy milk shakes.

What's brown, has two humps, and is found at the South Pole?
A lost camel.

What's brown, has three humps, and lives in the desert?
A camel with a rucksack.

How do you get down from a camel?
You don't – you get down from a duck.

What has four legs, two humps and flies?
A dead camel.

Cat jokes

What do you get if you cross a cat with a hammer, a saw and a spanner?
A tool kitty.

What do you call a bald Cheshire cat?
Yul Grinner.

What happened to the cat when it swallowed a ball of wool?
It had mittens.

What's furry, has whiskers, and chases outlaws?
A posse cat.

Who wrote 'Thoughts of a Chinese Cat'?
Chairman Miaow.

Chicken jokes

Why don't you ever see chickens in the zoo?
Because they can't afford the admission.

WENDY: Please, sir, my brother thinks he's a chicken.
TEACHER: *Well, why don't you take him to a doctor?*
WENDY: We can't do without the eggs.

What do you get if you cross a cockerel with a watch?
An alarm cluck.

What tells jokes and lays eggs?
A comedi-hen.

What do you call a chicken's ghost?
A poultrygeist.

Cow jokes

What do you get if you lie under a cow?
A pat on the head.

What do you get if you cross a cow with a duck?
Cream quackers.

What has four legs, two horns, and goes 'oom, oom'?
A cow walking backwards.

Why do cows lie down in the rain?
To keep each udder warm.

Knock, knock.
Who's there?
Chesterfield.
Chesterfield who?
Chesterfield full of cows, that's all.

Crab jokes

What do you get if you cross a crook with a crustacean?
A smash and crab raid.

Why was the crab arrested?
Because he was always pinching things.

Why did the ocean roar?
Because he had crabs in his bed.

What do you call a baby crab who won't share his toys?
Shellfish.

Crocodile jokes

What do you call a sick alligator?
An illigator.

What do you get if you cross a camera with a crocodile?
A snap shot.

What is a crocodile's favourite game?
Snap.

What do you get if you cross a crocodile with a rose?
I don't know, but I wouldn't try smelling it.

Dinosaur jokes

Why did the dinosaur cross the road?
Because there weren't any chickens in those days.

How do dinosaurs pass exams?
With extinction.

What would you get if you crossed a dinosaur with a witch?
A tyrannosaurus hex.

What's extinct and works in rodeos?
A bronco-saurus.

Dog jokes

What's got four legs, barks, and plays tennis?
John McEn-rover

Doctor, doctor, I think I'm a dog.
It's probably just your imagination, but until we're sure, get off my couch!

ALEX: Why did you buy a black and white dog?
FIONA: *The licence is cheaper.*

What do you get if you cross a dog with a test-tube?
A laboratory retriever.

What's got four legs, barks, and dances ballet?
Natalia Maka-rover

Donkey jokes

Why did the boy stand behind the donkey?
He thought he'd get a kick out of it.

What did the donkey say when he only had thistles to eat?
Thistle have to do.

Which key will open no door?
A donkey.

What's a stupid donkey?
An animal that makes an ass of itself.

Duck jokes

What do you get if you cross a duck and a genius?
A wise quacker.

Knock, knock.
Who's there?
Deduct.
Deduct who?
Donald Deduct!

What are ducks' favourite television programmes?
Duckumentaries.

What do you get if you cross a whale with a duckling?
Moby Duck.

'Doctor, doctor, I feel like a duck-doo.'
'What's a duck-doo?'
'Goes quack-quack, of course.'

The final mixed bag of jokes

What's a termite's favourite breakfast?
Oak meal.

What's white one minute and brown the next?
A white rat in a microwave.

What's brown one minute and white the next?
A brown rat in a deep freeze.

What's red, hunted, and blows up buildings?
Guy Fox.

A large sailing ship was at anchor off the coast of Mauritius, and two dodos watched as a group of sailors rowed ashore.
'We'd better hide,' said the first dodo.
'Why's that?' asked the second.
'Because we're supposed to be extinct, silly!'

A man got aboard a bus with a newt on his shoulder.
'What do you call him?' asked the conductor.
'Tiny,' replied the man.
'Why's that?'
'Because he's *my newt*, of course!'

Fishy knock knock jokes

Knock, knock.
Who's there?
Halibut.
Halibut who?
Halibut letting me in on the secret?

Knock, knock.
Who's there?
Tina.
Tina who?
Tina pilchards.

Knock, knock.
Who's there?
Kipper.
Kipper who?
Kipper hands to yourself!

Knock, knock.
Who's there?
Tuna.
Tuna who?
Tuna violin and it'll sound better.

Flea jokes

Did you hear about the incident at the flea circus?
A dog came along and stole the show.

Did you hear about the flea who failed his exams?
He didn't come up to scratch.

CUSTOMER: Waiter, there's a flea in my soup.
WAITER: *I'll tell him to hop it.*

How does a flea get from one place to another?
By itch-hiking.

What did one flea say to the other flea?
'Shall we walk or shall we take a dog?'

Fly jokes

What's the definition of insecticide?
A suicidal fly!

Knock, knock.
Who's there?
Jupiter.
Jupiter who?
Jupiter fly in my soup?

Two flies were sitting on Robinson Crusoe's head. 'Goodbye now,' one of them said. 'I'll see you on Friday.'

'I went fly-fishing yesterday.'
'Did you catch anything?'
'A four-pound bluebottle.'

Knock, knock.
Who's there?
Yul.
Yul who?
Yul catch more flies with honey than with vinegar.

Fly-in-my-soup jokes

'Waiter, waiter, there's a fly in my soup!'
'That's all right, sir, the spider will get it.'

'Waiter, waiter, there's a fly in my soup!'
'I know, it's the rotting meat that attracts them.'

'Waiter, waiter, there's a fly in my soup!'
'No, sir, that's the chef – the last customer was a witch doctor.'

'Waiter, waiter, there's a fly in my soup!'
'Don't worry, I'll send for the RSPCA.'

'Waiter, waiter, there's a fly in my soup!'
'If you throw it a pea it will play water polo.'

'Waiter, waiter, there's a fly in my soup!'
'I'm sorry, sir, the dog must have missed it.'

'Waiter, waiter, there's a fly in my soup!'
'Do keep quiet, or everyone will want one.'

'Waiter, waiter, there's a fly in my soup!'
'You'll have to get it out yourself, I can't swim.'

'Waiter, waiter, there's a fly in my soup!'
'If you leave it there the goldfish will get it.'

'Waiter, waiter, there's a fly in my soup!'
'Would you prefer it to be served separately?'

'Waiter, waiter, there's a fly in my soup!'
'Yes, sir, the chef used to be a tailor.'

'Waiter, waiter, there's a fly in my soup!'
'Yes, sir, they don't care what they eat, do they?'

Frog jokes

Where do frogs go if they have bad eyesight?
To a hoptician.

What's green inside and white outside, and squelchy to eat?
A frog sandwich.

What happens to frogs when they park on double yellow lines?
They get toad away.

What is green and hard?
A frog with a machine gun.

Giraffe jokes

What is worse than a giraffe with a sore throat?
A centipede with fallen arches.

Why is it so cheap to feed a giraffe?
A little goes a long way.

What's tall and smells nice?
A giraff-odil.

Does a giraffe get a sore throat if he gets his feet wet?
Yes, but not until two weeks later.

What do you get if you cross a racehorse with a giraffe?
An animal that's difficult to ride but great in a photo-finish.

Goat jokes

What's the best butter in the world?
A goat.

What's a neurotic young goat called?
A crazy mixed-up kid.

'Doctor, doctor, I feel like a goat.'
'How are the kids?'

'Doctor, doctor, I keep thinking I'm a goat.'
'Stop butting in while I'm talking.'

Goose jokes

What do cold geese suffer from?
Goose pimples.

Knock, knock.
Who's there?
Gander.
Gander who?
I be-Gander wander if you'd ever answer!

Why does a flight of geese follow a leading bird?
He's got the map.

What do geese eat?
Gooseberries.

What is the definition of a real goose?
Propaganda.

Gnu jokes

Why did the ant elope?
Nobody gnu.

Why did the zookeeper separate the gnus?
Because he had some good gnus and some bad gnus.

What do animals read in the zoo?
Gnus papers.

Where do gnus go for their holidays?
Gnu York.

There once was a gnu in the zoo
Who tired of the same daily view;
To seek a new sight
He stole out one night,
And where he went gnobody gnu.

Gorilla jokes

What do you do if you find a gorilla in your bed?
Sleep somewhere else.

What do you do if you want toast in the jungle?
Put some bread under the griller (gorilla!).

SID: I'm going to keep this gorilla under my bed.
BILL: *But what about the smell?*
SID: He'll just have to get used to it.

What is big and hairy and goes round and round?
A gorilla in a revolving door.

Hedgehog jokes

What do you get if you cross a porcupine with a skunk?
A smelly pincushion.

Why did the hedgehog cross the road?
To see his flat mate.

Why did the second hedgehog cross the road?
To pick up his squash partner.

What do you get if you cross a hedgehog with a stinging nettle?
Extremely sore hands!

Hippopotamus jokes

What's grey, heavy, and sends people to sleep?
A hypnopotamus.

What weighs over a ton and laughs a lot?
A happy potamus.

What do you get if you cross a hippo with someone who always feels ill?
A hippochondriac.

What weighs over a ton and jumps like a frog?
A hoppy potamus.

Horse jokes

Where do you take a sick horse?
To horsepital.

The saloon doors swung open. The cowboy rushed out, took a running jump, and landed flat on his face in the street.
'What's the matter, pardner?' asked the sheriff. 'Did they kick you out?'
'Nope,' said the cowboy, 'but I sure would like to get my hands on the varmint who moved my horse.'

What do you get if you cross a horse with a skunk?
Whinnie the Pooh.

What's brown and turns cartwheels?
A brown horse pulling a cart.

LOUISE: I went riding this morning.
ANNE: *Horseback?*
LOUISE: Yes, we came back together.

Insect jokes

'Doctor, doctor, I keep seeing this spinning insect.'
'Don't worry, it's just a bug that's going around.'

Knock, knock.
Who's there?
Weevil.
Weevil who?
Weevil work it out.

What do you call a new-born beetle?
A baby buggy.

Did you hear about the idiot caterpillar?
It turned into a frog!

What lies on the ground a hundred feet up?
A dead centipede.

CUSTOMER: Waiter, there's a dead beetle in my wine.
WAITER: *Well sir, you asked for something with a little body in it.*

Jokes from the fresh-water aquarium

'If there is no God,' said one goldfish to another, 'who changes our water?'

'This goldfish you sold me is always asleep.'
'That's not a goldfish, it's a kipper.'

Which fish go to heaven when they die?
Angel fish.

CUSTOMER: Waiter, this trout is bad.
WAITER (smacking fish): *You naughty, naughty trout.*

What's the fastest fish?
A motorpike.

Jokes from the sea aquarium

What fish terrorizes other fish?
Jack the Kipper.

What sits at the bottom of the sea and makes you an offer you can't refuse?
The Cod Father.

What leaves yellow footprints on the seabed?
A lemon sole.

BABY SARDINE: Mummy, what's a submarine?
MOTHER SARDINE: *It's just a tin of people, darling.*

Kangaroo jokes

When are kangaroos born?
In a leap year!

What do you get if you cross a kangaroo with a hippo?
Flat Australians!

Why do kangaroos hate rainy days?
Because the kids have to play indoors.

What do you call an exhausted kangaroo?
Out of bounds.

Leopard jokes

Why couldn't the leopard escape from the zoo?
Because he was always spotted.

The safari guide came running out of the jungle, into the game hunter's tent. 'I've just spotted a leopard,' he shouted.
'You can't fool me,' replied the hunter. 'They're born that way.'

What's yellow and black with red spots?
A leopard with measles.

SAFARI GUIDE: Quick, sir, shoot that leopard on the spot!
IDIOT HUNTER: *Be specific, you fool – which spot?*

Zoo library joke books

Swedish Lion Cubs by Bjorn Free
Wildlife Photography by Bill Dahide
Norwegian Animal Homes by Liv Ina Kennel
Snake Breeding by Anna Conda
Feeding Monkeys by P. Nuts
The Lion's Escape by Gaye Topen
Tiger Hunting by Claude Bottom
Better Pig Breeding by Lena Bacon
Milkman's Progress by Orson Cart
Off To Market – Tobias A. Pigg
Insect Life by Amos Quito
Chewing the Cud by Mike Howe
Three Bags Full by Barbara Blacksheep
Birdwatching by Jack Daw and Ray Venn
The Tea Party by Jim Pansy
Chasing Trappers by Chris Lee Bare
Who Killed Cock Robin? by Howard I. Know
The Dog Show by P. K. Knees
Crufts by G. Wah-Wah
Guard Dogs by Al Sayshun
Looking For Polar Bears by Ann Tarctic
Armour-plated Animals by Ahmed E. Lowe
Lazy Sloth by Eliza Sleep
Desert Crossing by Rhoda Camel
The Pleasures of Horse-riding by Jim Karna
Ten Years in the Ape House by Bab Boone
The Angry Lion by Claudia Armoff
Caring for Parrots by L. O. Polly
Feed Your Dog Properly by Norah Bone
Fighting Bulls By Matt Adore

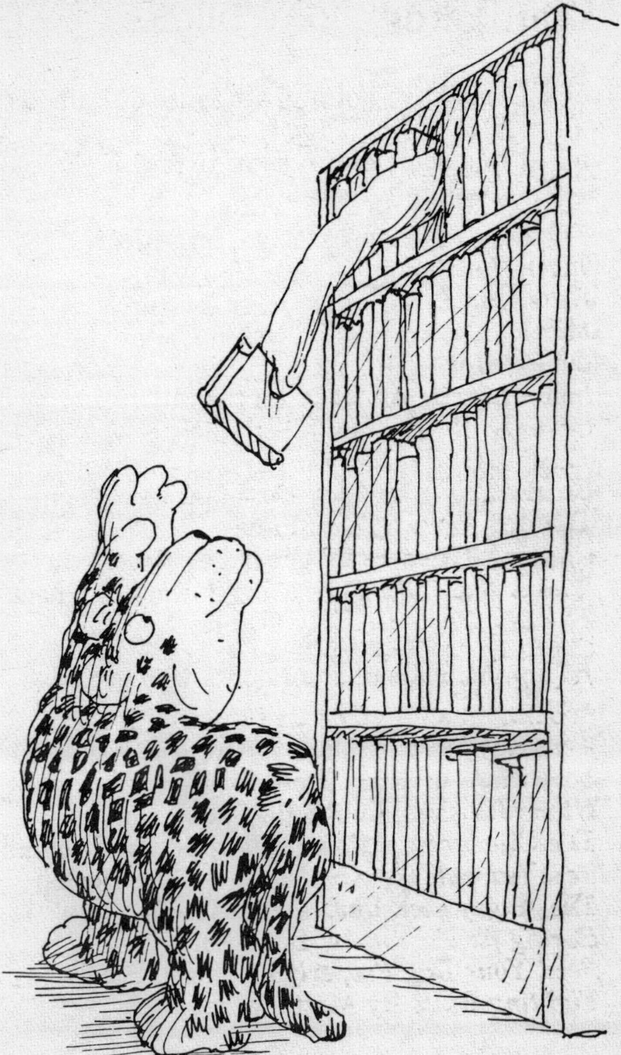

Lion jokes

JOHN: Lions have got a great sense of humour.
TRUDY: *How do you know?*
JOHN: I told some of my jokes to one at the zoo, and it absolutely roared!

Knock, knock.
Who's there?
Lionel.
Lionel who?
Lionel roar if you tread on his tail.

Knock, knock.
Who's there?
Aurora.
Aurora who?
Aurora is what a lion is!

Did you hear about the lioness who got towed away?
She parked on a yellow lion.

'What was the name of that chap who used to make his living sticking his right arm down a lion's throat?'
'I forget his name, but they call him 'Lefty' now . . .

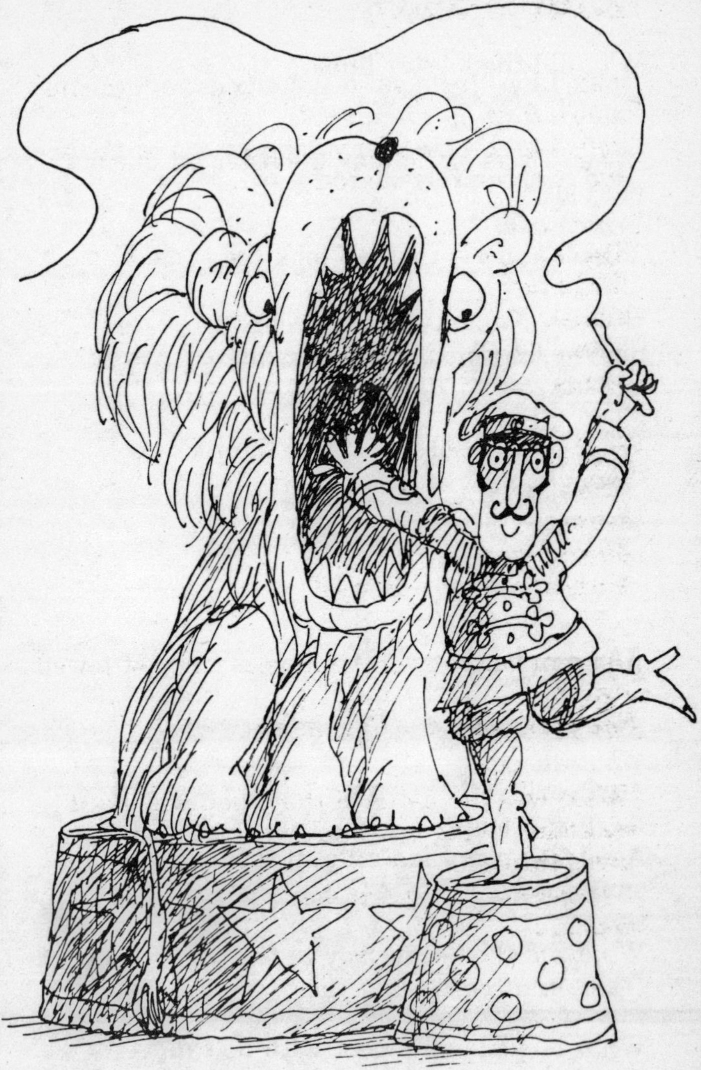

Lobster jokes

Why did the lobster blush?
Because the seaweed.

'When I was on holiday a lobster bit one of my toes.'
'Which one?'
'I don't know – they all look the same to me.'

TEACHER: Name two crustaceans.
IDIOT PUPIL: *Charing Crustacean and King's Crustacean.*

What did the lobster say to the rock-pool?
'Show us your mussels!'

Mixed bag

Knock, knock.
Who's there?
Aardvark.
Aardvark who?
Aardvark a million miles, for one of your smiles . . .

What did the beaver say to the tree?
It's been nice gnawing you.

What do you call a deer with no eye?
No idea.

Knock, knock.
Who's there?
Tilly.
Tilly who?
I didn't know you were a foxhunter!

Mole jokes

What do you get if you cross a mole with a hedgehog?
Tunnels that leak.

What purrs along the motorway and leaves holes in the lawn?
A Moles Royce.

How do you stop moles digging holes in your lawn?
Hide their spades.

What is a mole after it's four weeks old?
Five weeks old.

What do moles have that no other animal has?
Baby moles.

Monkey jokes

What do you call a monkey with a sweet tooth?
A meringue-outang.

What did the monkey say as he fell out of the tree?
'AARRGGHH!'

What do you get if you cross a spanner with a chimpanzee?
A monkey wrench.

Where do baby monkeys sleep?
In apricots.

Moose jokes

What does a moose read on the train?
A moosepaper.

What's got antlers and sucks an awful lot of blood?
A moose-quito.

What's the biggest moose in the world?
A hippopotamoose.

In what American state are there the most moose?
Moosouri.

What Russian moose was a famous composer?
Moosorgski.

Mosquito jokes

What wears a black cape, flies around at night, and sucks people's blood?
A mosquito wearing a black cape.

What is the difference between a man bitten by a mosquito and a man going on holiday?
One is going to itch, the other is itching to go.

What has six legs, bites, and talks in code?
A morse-quito.

What is a mosquito's favourite sport?
Skin-diving.

Moth and butterfly jokes

FIRST MOTH: I don't think much of our new neighbour.
SECOND MOTH: *Nor do I – she picks holes in everything.*

Why couldn't the butterfly go to the ball?
Because it was a mothball.

Why did the butterfly?
Because it saw the milk-float.

Which insect eats the least?
The moth – it just eats holes.

What is a myth?
A female moth.

Mouse jokes

What's a mouse's favourite game?
Hide and squeak.

What's grey, buzzes, and eats cheese?
A mouse-quito.

What's grey, has twelve legs, and can't see?
Three blind mice.

What's grey, squeaks, and hangs around in caves?
Stalagmice.

What do you call a thin mouse?
A narrow squeak.

Noah's Ark jokes

How did Noah manage in the dark?
He turned on the floodlights.

Did everything go into the Ark in pairs?
No, the maggots went in the apples.

Where did Noah keep his bees?
In Ark-hives.

Knock, knock.
Who's there?
Noah.
Noah who?
Noah bargain when I see one.

Not-the-animals-you-expected jokes

What has one horn and gives milk?
A milk delivery van.

What runs but has no legs?
A tap.

What has a neck but no head?
A bottle.

What has two legs, one wheel, and smells?
A wheelbarrow full of manure.

What do you get hanging from trees?
Sore arms.

What's boring and moves from branch to branch carrying a briefcase?
A bank manager.

Octopus jokes

What do you call a neurotic octopus?
A crazy mixed-up squid.

What do you get if you cross eight arms with a watch?
A clocktopus.

What's wet and says 'How do you do?' sixteen times?
Two octopusses shaking hands.

Who snatched the baby octopus and held it to ransom?
Squidnappers.

Why did the man cross a chicken with an octopus?
So all the family could have a leg each.

Owl jokes

What do lovesick owls say when it's raining?
Too-wet-to-woo.

OWL: Us owls are a lot wiser than you chickens.
CHICKEN: *Oh yeah? What makes you so sure?*
OWL: Did you ever hear of Kentucky Fried Owl?

What did the owl and the goat do at the square dance?
The hootenanny.

What sits in a tree and says, 'Hoots mon, hoots mon'?
A Scottish owl.

Parrot jokes

What is a Macaw?
A Scottish parrot.

What do you stuff dead parrots with?
Polyfilla.

What do you get if you cross a parrot with a watch?
Politics.

MAN: Can I have a parrot for my son, please?
PET SHOP OWNER: I'm sorry, sir, we don't do swops.

Who has a parrot that shouts 'Pieces of four!'?
Short John Silver.

Penguin jokes

What goes black and white, black and white, black and white, black and white?
A penguin rolling down a hill.

What do you get if you cross a penguin with a sheep?
A sheepskin dinner jacket.

What bird can write underwater?
A ballpoint penguin.

What's black and white and makes a dreadful noise?
A penguin playing the bagpipes.

What's black and white and goes round and round?
A penguin in a revolving door.

Pig jokes

What's a pig's favourite ballet?
Swine Lake.

What do you get if you cross a pig with a motorway?
A road hog.

What's creamy and good for sick pigs?
Oinkment.

What's pink, has four legs, and plays football?
Queen's Pork Rangers.

Polar bear jokes

What is big, white and found in the desert?
A lost polar bear.

What's white, furry, and smells of peppermint?
A Polo bear.

'Mummy,' said the baby polar bear, 'am I one hundred per cent pure polar bear?'
'Of course you are, son,' said his mother. 'Why do you ask?'
'Because I'm flippin' freezing!'

Why do polar bears have fur coats?
They'd look silly in tweed ones!

Rabbit jokes

What did the rabbit want to do when he grew up?
Join the Hare Force.

Knock, knock.
Who's there?
Rabbit.
Rabbit who?
Rabbit up nicely, it's a present.

What does Bugs Bunny use when he goes fishing?
A hare net.

DICK: Why do you call your car 'Bunny'?
DIANE: *Because I only use if for short hops.*

What do you get if you cross an insect and a rabbit?
Bugs Bunny.

Rhinoceros jokes

What's as big as a rhinoceros and weighs nothing?
A rhinoceros's shadow.

What should you do if you see an angry rhino?
Hope he doesn't see you!

FIRST RHINO: What is that creature over there?
SECOND RHINO: *It's a hippopotamus.*
FIRST RHINO: Fancy having to live with an ugly face like that!

TEACHER: Where are rhinos found?
PUPIL: *Please, miss, rhinos are so large, they hardly ever get lost.*

TEACHER: What family does the rhinoceros belong to?
PUPIL: *I don't know, miss — nobody in our street has one.*

Sea mammal jokes

Knock, knock.
Who's there?
Walrus.
Walrus who?
Do you walrus ask such silly questions?

Who is the Lord Privy Seal?
A noble animal like a sealion, who lives in a lavatory.

What do you call angry dolphins?
Cross porpoises.

What do sea monsters eat?
Fish and ships.

Shark jokes

What do you get if you cross a shark with a snowman?
Frost-bite.

What do you get if you cross an American president with a shark?
Jaws Washingon.

What do you get if you cross a shark with the Loch Ness monster?
Loch Jaws!

What happened to the yacht that sank in shark-infested waters?
It came back with a skeleton crew.

Sheep jokes

CUSTOMER: Do you serve lamb?
WAITER: *I'm sorry, sir, we don't allow animals to dine here.*

What do sheep look for at the sales?
Baagains.

What keeps sheep warm in winter?
Central bleating.

Why was the sheep arrested by the motorway police?
For making a ewe turn.

What's white and goes 'Baa-baa-splat'?
A sheep falling off a cliff.

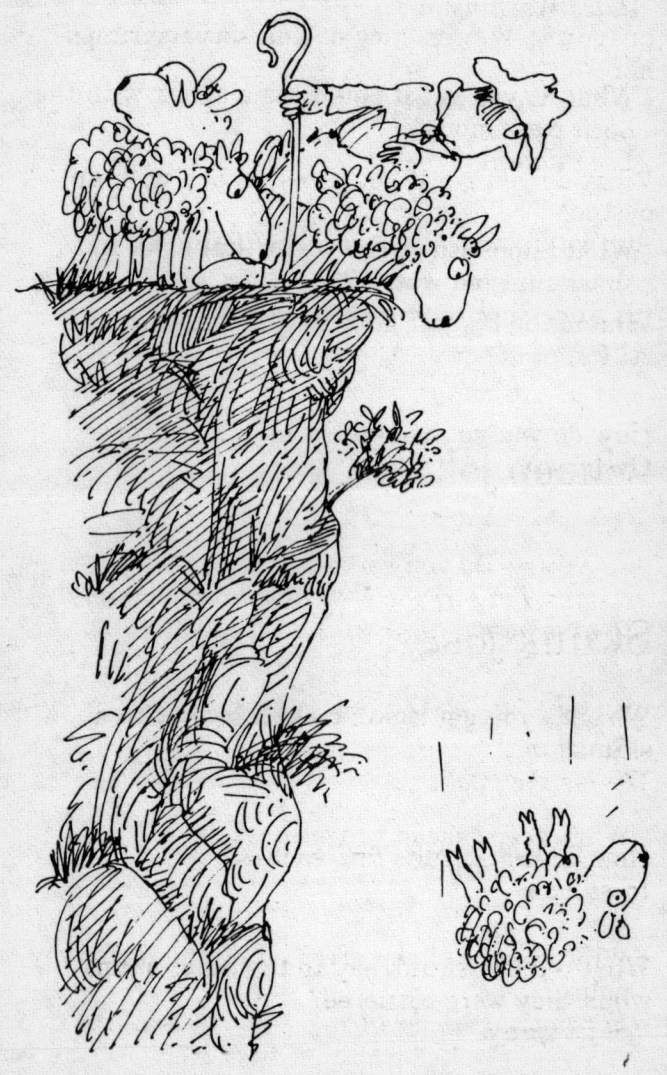

Shellfish jokes

CUSTOMER: Waiter, how do you serve shrimps here?
WAITER: *We bend down.*

What do you get if you cross an owl with an oyster?
A creature that drops pearls of wisdom.

Who is the biggest gangster in the sea?
Al Caprawn.

How do you get a shellfish up a mountain?
Oyster up.

Skunk jokes

What do you get if you cross a bear with a skunk?
Winnie the Pooh.

How do lost skunks find each other?
In stink.

What did one skunk say to the other skunk when they were cornered?
'Let us spray.'

What did the forgetful skunk say when the wind changed?
'It's all coming back to me now.'

What do you get if you cross a skunk with an eagle?
An animal that stinks to high heaven.

Slug and snail jokes

CUSTOMER: Have you ever been to the zoo?
WAITER: *No, sir – why?*
CUSTOMER: You'd get quite a kick at the speed of the snails zipping by.

What happens when snails have a fight?
They slug it out.

PUPIL: Are slugs nice to eat, miss?
TEACHER: *Don't talk about such disgusting things at the lunch table. Get on with your meal and keep quiet.*
(After lunch)
TEACHER: *Now, what was all that about slugs?*
PUPIL: Oh, it doesn't matter, miss. There was one in your salad, but it's gone now.

How do snails get their shells shiny?
They use snail varnish.

Snake jokes

BOY SNAKE: Dad, are we poisonous?
FATHER SNAKE: *Of course we are, son – why do you ask?*
BOY SNAKE: Because I've just bitten my tongue.

What do you call a snake that works for the government?
A civil serpent.

Which snake is good at maths?
An adder!

What happens when you put snakes on a car window?
You get windscreen vipers.

Spider jokes

Knock, knock.
Who's there?
Spider.
Spider who?
Spider when she thought I wasn't looking.

Where do spiders live?
Crawley.

Where do spiders play football?
At Webley.

What's a spider that has just got married?
A newly-web.

What was the spider doing in the bowl of alphabet soup?
Learning to read.

Squirrel jokes

What sort of animals use nut-crackers?
Toothless squirrels.

What do squirrels have when they find some nuts?
A cracking good time.

Where do squirrels go when they have nervous breakdowns?
To the nuthouse.

How do you catch a squirrel?
Act like a nut.

What did the squirrel say to his girlfriend?
'I'm nuts about you.'

Tiger jokes

What do you get if you cross a plum with a tiger?
A purple people-eater.

'Who went into a lion's den and came out alive?'
'*Daniel.*'
'Who went into a tiger's den and came out alive?'
'*I don't know.*'
'The tiger!'

What did the idiot call his pet tiger?
Spot.

What's the best way to talk to a man-eating tiger?
By long-distance telephone.

'Have you ever seen a man-eating tiger?'
'No, but I once saw a man eating chicken.'

Turkey jokes

Why did the turkey cross the road?
To prove he wasn't chicken.

Where do all good turkeys go when they die?
To oven.

NOAH: I thought we had two turkeys when we set sail?
MRS NOAH: *Well, dear, it is Christmas. . .*

Why is a turkey like an evil little creature?
Because it's always a-gobblin'.

The mother turkey was scolding her children for being naughty. 'You bad children,' she said, 'if your father could see you he'd turn over in his gravy . . .'

Turtle jokes

Why did the tortoise beat the hare?
Nothing goes faster than Shell.

What's a tortoise?
It's what the teacher did.

What do rich turtles wear?
People-neck sweaters.

What was the tortoise doing on the motorway?
About one mile an hour.

PATIENT: Doctor, doctor, I keep thinking I'm a tortoise!
DOCTOR: *Never mind, we'll soon have you out of your shell.*

Underwater jokes

What lies at the bottom of the sea and wobbles?
A jelly fish.

What lies at the bottom of the sea and shivers?
A nervous wreck.

What does an electric eel taste like?
Shocking.

What's a mermaid?
A deep-she fish.

Wasp jokes

What is a wasp?
An insect that stings for its supper.

Where do wasps come from?
Stingapore.

What do you do with a sick wasp?
Take it to waspital.

If we get honey from a bee, what do we get from a wasp?
Waspberry jam.

Where do wasps wait for transport?
At a buzz-stop.

CUSTOMER: What's the meaning of this dead wasp in my soup?
WAITER: *I don't know, sir, I don't tell fortunes.*

Whale jokes

What do you call a baby whale?
A little squirt.

What do you call a baby whale that's crying?
A little blubber.

What do you get if you cross a whale with a nun?
Blubber and sister.

Where do you weigh a whale?
At a whale-weigh station.

Who's zoo

Antelope: When two ants run away to get married.
Battery hen: A chicken that lays electric eggs.
Caterpillar: An upholstered worm.
Dachshund: Half a dog high by a dog and a half long.
Earwig: False hair worn over the ears.
Fleece: Insects that get into dirty animals' hair.
Goblet: A baby turkey.
Hogwash: A pig's laundry.
Illegal: A sick bird.

Jitterbug: A nervous insect.
Kettle: A water 'otter.
Lobster: A tennis player.
Mosquito: A flying hypodermic needle.
Nightingale: A very windy evening.
Octopus: An eight-sided cat.
Perch: A fish found in a bird cage.
Quack: A doctor who treats sick ducks.
Robin: A bird that steals.
Slug: A homeless snail.
Timber wolf: An animal with wooden legs.
Unicorn: A horse that eats ice cream cones through the top of its head.
Vulture: A bird you hope won't drop in for dinner.
Watchdog: An animal that goes tick-tick-woof, tick-tick-woof.
Xylophone: A telephone belonging to Mr Xylo, the zookeeper.
Yak: The most talkative animal on earth.
Zebra: A horse with venetian blinds.

Wolf jokes

Why are wolves like cards?
They come in packs.

Which animal has wooden legs?
A timber wolf.

Who shouted 'Knickers!' at the big bad wolf?
Little Rude Riding Hood.

What's the difference between a wolf and a flea?
One howls on the prairie, and the other prowls on the hairy.

Worm jokes

What did the woodworm say when he went into the pub?
'Is the bar tender here?'

A worm received an invitation to a party in a field of corn. It went in one ear and out the other.

BOY: I was eating an apple, and I swallowed a worm.
DOCTOR: *Goodness! Let me give you something for it.*
BOY: No thanks – I'll just let it starve.

Did you hear about the stupid woodworm?
It was found in a brick!

How did the glow-worm feel when he was stepped on?
De-lighted.

Yet another mixed bag of jokes

What do you do with a wombat?
Play wom, of course!

What is the difference between a weasel and a stoat?
One is weasily recognized, and the other is stoatally different.

What happened when two American stoats got married?
They became the United Stoats of America.

Where do hamsters come from?
Hamsterdam.

What is brown, hairy, dangerous, and lives in Tibet?
Yak the Ripper.

Zebra jokes

What is black and white and red all over?
A sunburnt zebra.

What do you get if you cross a zebra with a pig?
Striped sausages.

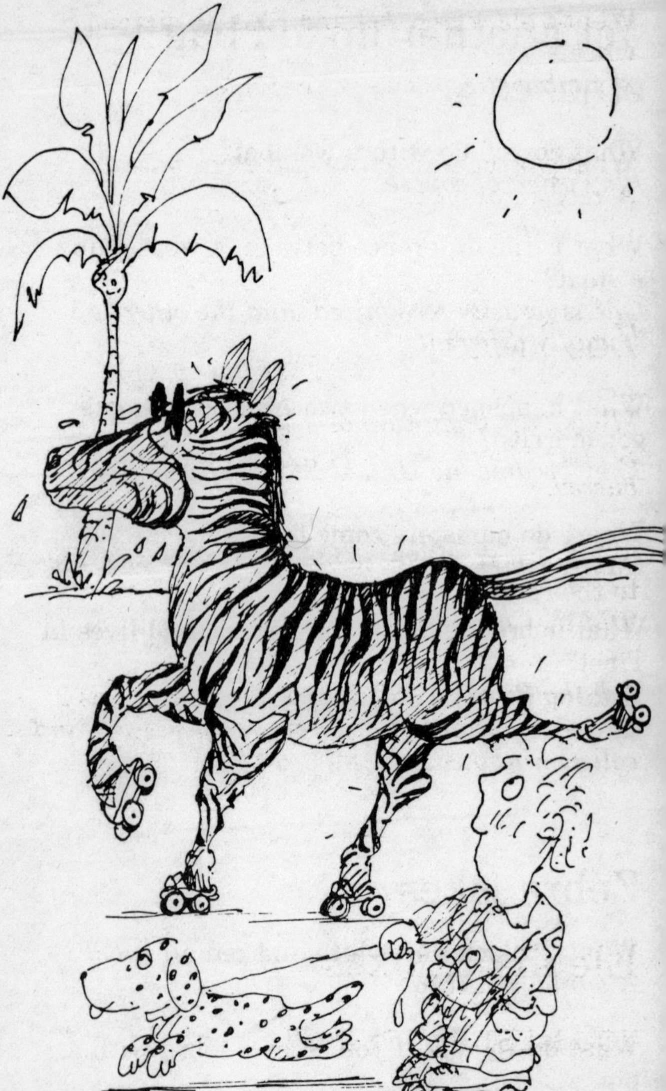

What's black and red and runs on sixteen wheels?
A sunburnt zebra on roller-skates.

What's black and white and stops buses?
A zebra crossing.

Zoo jokes

What's the definition of a zoo?
A place where people go but animals are barred.

'When I was six years old my father took me to the zoo.'
'Did they accept you?'

'I thing I'll take our Jimmy to the zoo today.'
'If they want the little devil, let them come and collect him themselves.'

Elephant jokes

YOU MUST BE JOKING!!

More Beaver Books

On the following pages you will find some other exciting Beaver Books to look out for in your local bookshop

JOKE BOOKS

If you enjoyed reading all the hilarious jokes in this book, perhaps you ought to try some more of our zany joke books. They are available in bookshops or they can be ordered directly from us. Just complete the form below and enclose the right amount of money and the books will be sent to you at home.

☐ THE WOOLLY JUMPER JOKE BOOK	Peter Eldin	£1.25
☐ MORE BROWNIE JOKES		£1.25
☐ THE WOBBLY JELLY JOKE BOOK	Jim Eldridge	£1.25
☐ A VERY MICE JOKE BOOK	John Hegarty	£1.25
☐ THE JOKE-A-DAY FUN BOOK	Janet Rogers	£1.50
☐ THE CRAZY JOKE BOOK STRIKES BACK	Janet Rogers	£1.50
☐ THE ELEPHANT JOKE BOOK	Katie Wales	£1.00
☐ FLOELLA'S FUNNIEST JOKES	Floella Benjamin	£1.25

If you would like to order books, please send this form, and the money due to:
ARROW BOOKS, BOOKSERVICE BY POST, PO BOX 29, DOUGLAS, ISLE OF MAN, BRITISH ISLES. Please enclose a cheque or postal order made out to Arrow Books Ltd for the amount due including 30p per book for postage and packing both for orders within the UK and for overseas orders.

NAME ....

ADDRESS ....

....

Please print clearly.